Whittling the Country Bear
& His Friends

12 Simple Projects for Beginners

Mike Shipley

FOX CHAPEL
PUBLISHING

Acknowledgments

Thanks to Sherry for always giving positive support. Thanks to my three girls for giving me those grandbabies.

To learn more about the other great books from Fox Chapel Publishing, or to find a retailer near you, call toll-free 800-457-9112 or visit us at *www.FoxChapelPublishing.com*.

We are always looking for talented authors. To submit an idea, please send a brief inquiry to acquisitions@foxchapelpublishing.com.

Printed in Malaysia
Second printing

Table of Contents

ABOUT THE AUTHOR 4

INTRODUCTION 5

Part One: Getting Started 7

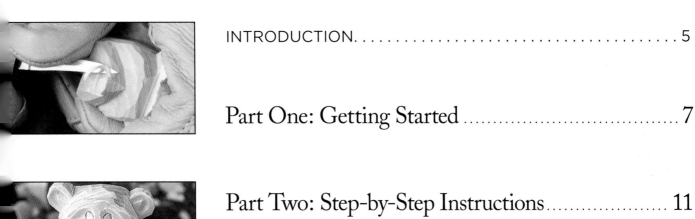

Part Two: Step-by-Step Instructions 11
Carving Barry the Bear 12
Painting Barry the Bear 24
Antiquing Barry the Bear 28

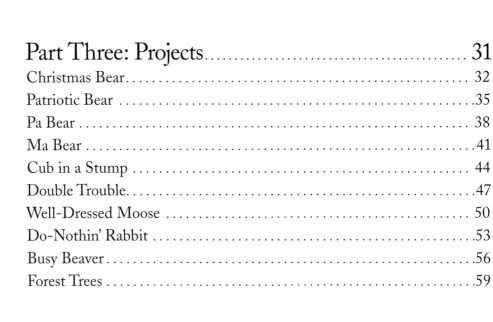

Part Three: Projects 31
Christmas Bear 32
Patriotic Bear 35
Pa Bear 38
Ma Bear 41
Cub in a Stump 44
Double Trouble 47
Well-Dressed Moose 50
Do-Nothin' Rabbit 53
Busy Beaver 56
Forest Trees 59

About the Author

Thank you for the investment of your time and money in the purchase of this book. I appreciate woodcarving books very much, and I buy a lot of them. In fact, that's how I started carving about 27 years ago. I bought a book, a knife, and a blank, and I started a learning process that is still going today. At the time I thought I couldn't really afford to spend hard earned money on such things, but what a wise investment that initial purchase was! And that's not because of any money I've made since, but because of the pure enjoyment and satisfaction of holding a finished woodcarving in my hands. Back in the old days, there weren't many woodcarving books available. Today we have a long list of books to choose from, and I'm happy you've chosen this one. I hope this book will be the beginning of years of enjoyment for you.

—Mike Shipley

Introduction

Whittling these woodland animals has been a good experience for me because I stepped out of my carving "comfort zone." Anyone who is acquainted with my work knows that I like to carve Santas, snowmen, and hillbillies in a moderate caricature style. In fact, that's what I always teach: To improve your carving and gain confidence, you need to carve what you like and what you are most comfortable with. But every carver needs to step out of that carving comfort zone every now and then just to stretch his or her talents a little bit.

These animals were quite a stretch for me, and I learned a lot by carving something different. The pieces in this book are not intended to be realistic animals.

I used a moderate caricature style to make these forest creatures slightly humorous and to exaggerate them to the point where the viewer knows they are not intended to be realistic. A caricature carving can range from only slight exaggeration to exteme exaggeration, so my description of the process in this book would be moderate exaggeration.

I designed each project to be fairly easy and enjoyable to carve. As I always tell my students: Add enough detail to make it interesting; keep it simple enough to make it fun.

I hope you enjoy this unusual bunch of characters.

—Mike Shipley

Ma and Pa are proud of their bear cubs, despite the endless trouble their children seem to get themselves into. (Ma Bear pattern, page 42; Double Trouble pattern, page 48; Pa Bear pattern, page 39.)

The bear cubs in Barry the Bear's forest are carved in the same manner. The single bear cub in the tree stump is much easier to carve than the two bears and their hidden friend. (Cub in a Stump pattern, page 45; Double Trouble pattern, page 48; Forest Trees pattern, pages 60 and 61.)

Busy Beaver and Do-Nothin' Rabbit are just two of the many friends Barry the Bear has in his forest home. (Busy Beaver pattern, page 57; Do-Nothin' Rabbit pattern, page 54.)

The three bears in this photograph are all cut from the same basic pattern. Simple alterations from the hats on the Christmas Bear to the Patriotic Bear. The steps for carving and painting Barry the Bear are demonstrated in the step-by-step instruction section of this book. (Christmas Bear pattern page 33; Patriotic Bear pattern, page 36; Barry the Bear pattern, page 13.)

Part One

Getting Started

The projects in this book can be carved with a basic set of woodcarving tools, including a detail knife, a knife with a 2" (5cm) blade, several gouges and a V-tool. See the materials list at the beginning of each project for a list of tools specific to that project.

Choosing and sharpening tools

Carving or whittling small projects like these doesn't require a lot of complicated tools. I used about 12 different knives and gouges to carve the projects in this book. The two basic tools that I depend on are a good bench knife with a blade length of 1½" to 2" (4 to 5cm) and a ⁵⁄₁₆" (8mm) V-tool. I use the knife often, but I also do quite a bit of work with the V-tool. With a little practice you can do a lot of work with the V-tool that you might normally do with the knife. Always try to do as much work as possible with one tool before you reach for the next tool.

There are many tools and sharpening devices on the market today. I prefer a tool without a beveled blade. In other words, I want the blade of my knife, gouge, or V-tool to come down in a flat wedge to the cutting edge. A beveled tool will have a gentle slope with a steeper slope closer to the cutting edge of the blade. A beveled tool is probably safer and less aggressive, but it causes you

to apply more force to cut the wood, thereby slowing you down.

I would much rather spend time carving than sharpening, so I use a 1" (2.5cm) wide belt sander with a 300 or 400 grit belt to sharpen my knife blade. This method is pretty aggressive, but it's fast and easy. I carefully lay the blade flat on the belt to grind any bevel to a flat surface all the way to the cutting edge. After I remove the bevel, I simply buff the blade with a cotton buffing wheel on a standard bench grinder. If you are unfamiliar with this sharpening technique, take it slow at first and realize that you might need a little practice. Avoid pushing too hard on the blade. Too much pressure will quickly heat the metal to a point where it will turn a darker color. When that happens, the temper in the metal is ruined and you will have to grind the darkened metal away before making another attempt to sharpen the blade.

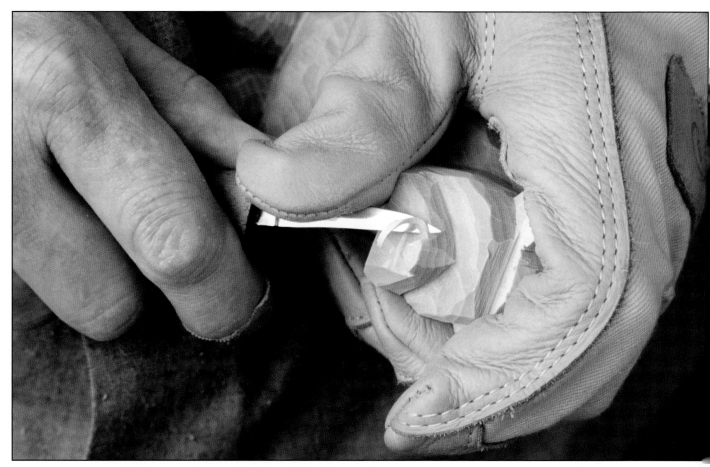

Placing the thumb of the hand that holds the piece behind the thumb of the hand that holds the knife will give you extra control as you make precise cuts.

Carving tips

If you are a beginning carver, you may notice that you are making those small, cautious cuts about the size of a speck of sawdust. That's a natural tendency for a beginner. You are being careful not to cut away too much wood or to cut off the wrong thing. While good for building confidence, those small cuts usually result in a finished piece that is blocky or flat, or where the basic dimensions are "off" or distorted.

The only way to stop making small, cautious cuts is to practice. Now I know you probably get tired of hearing that word, but more carving is the only way to gain the confidence to make the bigger, necessary cuts, which is the only way to overcome the "sawdust syndrome." Remember, as you carve, you want to be removing nice big chips of wood, not sawdust. You will find that the bigger cuts will speed up your carving time, as well as give the finished piece a much more natural look. Using larger tools will help with making the bigger cuts. I use the largest tool possible, and of course tool size will depend on size of the piece, but as a rule always use the largest tool possible.

Good, clean cuts are also a must. Where one area stops and another begins—an arm resting against the body, for example—I use a good, sharp V-tool. Make the cuts in those dividing areas clean, even if you have to use a knife tip. In addition to making the carving look cleaner, clean cuts will also help to stop the acrylic paint colors from blending together when you paint the finished piece.

The ability to make clean cuts is part practice and part know-how. In the step-by-step photos, notice how I sometimes plant my thumb on my carving hand and how

use my thumb on my left hand. This is for tool control. Never make a cut without knowing how deep or how far that cut is going to go. The proper use of the thumb controls the pressure on the blade's cutting edge.

Choosing wood

use basswood for all of the projects in this book. asswood is a tight-grained wood that does not split or plinter. It is a soft wood, making it ideal for hand carving. asswood can be purchased though mail order services or your local carving supply store. Always choose basswood hat is light in color and light in weight; the lighter the etter in both cases. Avoid using any basswood blocks that now dark streaks, knots, or other surface imperfections.

Good lighting is a must. I have a 48" (122cm) florescent shop light over my workstation, and it seems to provide good general lighting without shadow. Direct lighting such as a standard light bulb seems to cast shadow. Poor lighting can affect your work, and you may not even be aware of it.

Transferring the pattern to your block of wood can be easily done with a piece of carbon paper and a stylus or a pounce wheel. Simply place the carbon paper between the wood and the pattern, carbon side down, and trace over the outline of the pattern. You'll notice that the front view pattern and one of the side view patterns in this book are outlined with a dashed line. This line indicates the band saw cut line. A disc sander can be used to remove excess wood from the band sawed blank.

I prefer using carbon paper to transfer the pattern on to a thicker paper such as poster board, then cut the silhouette out with scissors. The silhouette is all that I need when band sawing a pattern.

If you are fortunate enough to have sketching or drawing abilities, this will be a big plus in your carving. I have never been able to draw well, so I don't rely on having the perfect pattern. Before I start any carving I have all of the features and details of the piece in mind but, of course, having a well designed pattern in front of you will only help.

When I transfer the pattern to the wood, I concentrate on well-proportioned side and front view silhouettes.

Then I carve the details to fit the proportions that I've sawed with the band saw. Correct beginning proportions are critical: A good finished piece comes from a well proportioned blank.

It is possible to finish a piece from a blank with a few distinctive features sawed in with the band saw, and you could even start with a square blank of wood, but you will need to do a lot of extra work to remove the excess wood. Removing too much excess wood is distracting and it's hard work. Removing the right amount of wood with the band saw is a real time saver.

Part Two

Step-by-Step Instructions

The step-by-step demonstration on the following pages focuses on the biggest guy in the forest, Barry the Bear. Barry is quite the ham and is quite accustomed to having his picture taken.

From the carver's perspective, learning to carve, paint, and stain Barry will teach you all the techniques you'll need to know to finish the other projects in this book.

As you work through the step-by-step demonstration, be sure to concentrate on duplicating the cuts and paint strokes as they are shown in the photographs. If you are a beginning carver, this is especially important. If you come across a cut that seems awkward to you, practice making that cut on a separate piece of wood before trying it on your in-progress piece. Similarly, if you are unfamiliar with a carving tool, practice using it on a separate piece of wood until you are comfortable with the motions and control needed to properly use the tool. Painting techniques are always best practiced before they are applied. Make sure that you are happy with the colors before you add them to your carving.

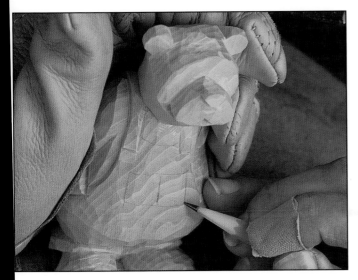

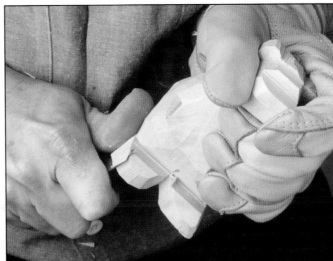

Carving Barry the Bear

Barry the Bear is just a laid-back, lazy bear. He has never punched a time clock in his life. He's "bearly" up by noon, but that's all right with him. He doesn't even care if you call him lazy, just as long as you call him at dinnertime because missing a meal is one thing that he just couldn't bear.

To carve Barry you will need a block of basswood 2½" (6.5cm) wide by 2⅜" (6cm) thick by 5" (12.5cm) tall.

Barry the Bear

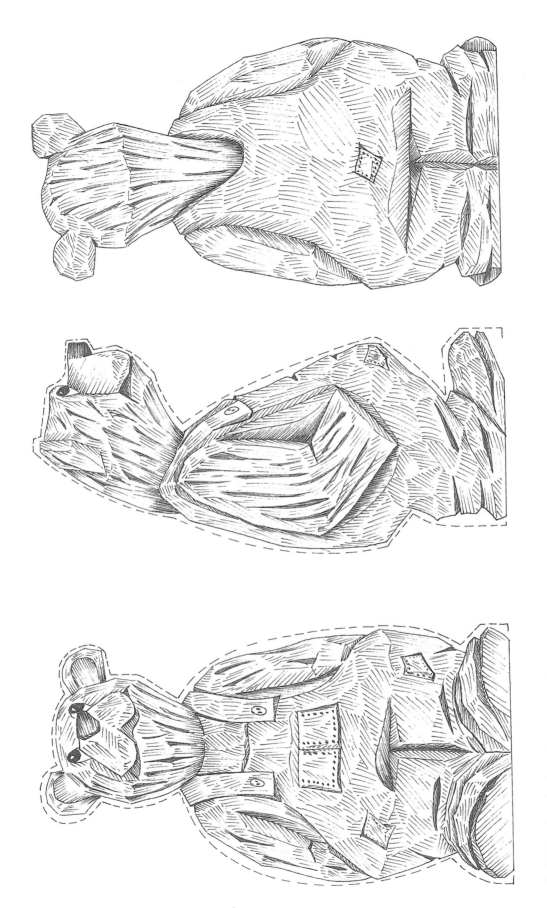

Materials List: Carving

- Band saw (optional)
- Disc sander (optional)
- Basswood block, 2½" x 2⅜" x 5" (6.5 x 6 x 12.5cm) tall
- Pencil
- Carving glove
- ⅛" (3mm) U-gouge
- Detail knife
- Carving knife with a 2" (5cm) blade
- ⅜" (10mm) V-tool
- ⁵⁄₁₆" (8mm) V-tool
- ⅛" (4mm) V-tool
- 220-grit sandpaper

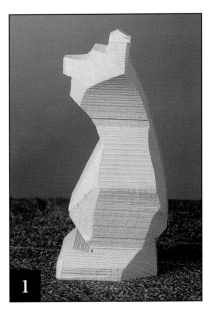

Transfer the side view band saw pattern to the basswood block. The grain will run the length of the block. Using a band saw or coping saw, cut the side view first. Leave the wood intact on the back of the head to stabilize the block on the saw table.

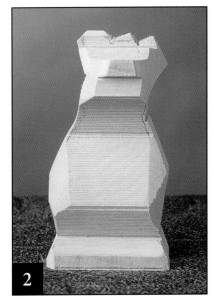

Transfer the front view band saw pattern to the front of the block. After sawing the front view, remove the unwanted wood on the back of the head that was left to stabilize the block. I also use a disc sander with a very coarse disc to round some of the edges and to remove a littl of the excess wood that won't be needed

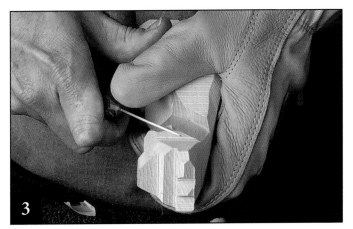

Transfer the carving pattern to the block. On any piece I always start by shaping and sizing the head. In this photograph I'm trimming the head and neck width.

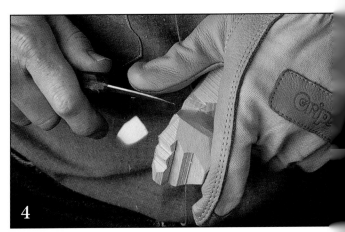

Because of the grain, I'm cutting down to the shoulder.

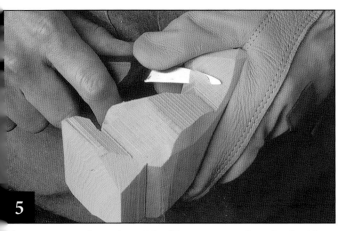

5

Now move to the other side. Remove wood on both sides until the head and neck widths are established. Keep in mind that the neck thins down as it nears the body. The width of the neck is much smaller at the body than at the main head area.

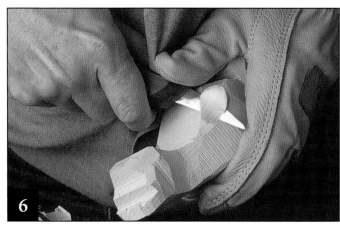

6

After working the neck down to the body, start rounding the body. For this step, I'm using a good, hefty knife with a 2" (5cm) blade. Simply round the front of the body by carving away the sawed wood.

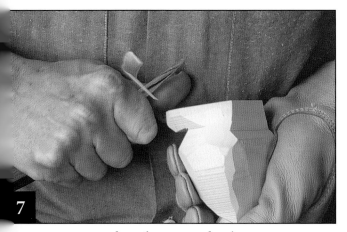

7

Remove some wood on the area under the arms.

8

Move to the other side and clean up the pants and lower legs by rounding and removing the sawed wood.

9

With the body slightly rounded, use a pencil to sketch the arm lines.

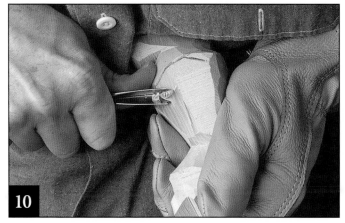

10

Use a ⅜" (10mm) V-tool to cut the pencil lines and deepen the cuts. Remove wood on the body and the arms by tilting the V-tool to either side, using the side of the tool as if it were a knife.

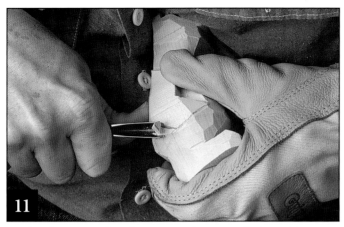

11

Make the cut under the arm in the same fashion. Deepen it to raise the arm. Clean up the body area next to the arm to raise the arm away from the body.

12

Clean up the body and the arms with the knife. Slope the pants down to where the pant leg stops. Make the same cuts on the other leg.

13

Now check the body and the arms for good proportion. To match the arms, look straight at the piece. Look at how one arm bends and compare it to the other. Use a V-tool or knife for any adjustments you need to make to match the arms.

14

Use the knife to remove wood on both sides of the head in front of the ears. Notice how I'm using my left thumb to help control the knife blade. As you work the head down to size, be careful of the ears; they are getting thinner and more fragile with every cut.

15

Take a close look at the bear's head in this photograph. Notice the work done on the head. Next draw a centerline on the boots with a pencil.

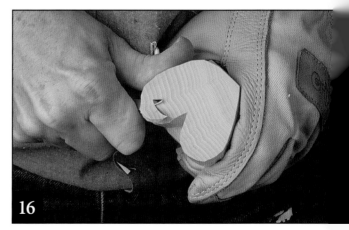

16

With the knife, cut the centerline. Start rounding the boot toes and separating the boot tips.

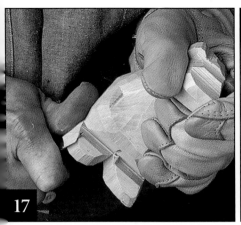

17

Continue rounding the boots. Work them down to a suitable size. Keep in mind that the boots can be a little oversized; they are intended to appear large and comical.

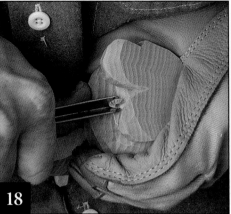

18

While shaping the boots, I made a cut under the boots to raise the boot toes slightly. Now mark the centerline of the legs and use the 5⁄16" (8mm) V-tool to cut the line. This is just a simple, deep cut in front and in back to distinguish the legs.

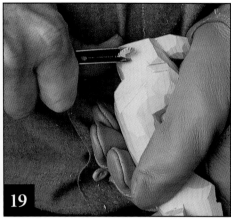

19

Using the same V-tool, cut the pant cuffs around the bottom of the pant legs.

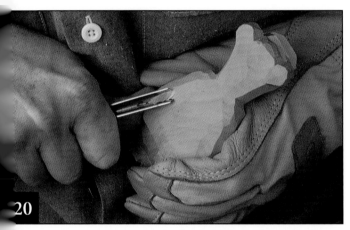

20

Now cut the arm lines on the back of the piece. Use the sides of the V-tool to round the arm and body areas next to this cut.

21

Now, with the hard work out of the way, draw the cheek lines. Notice the raised eyebrow. Start the line at the brow and continue straight down on both sides of the face.

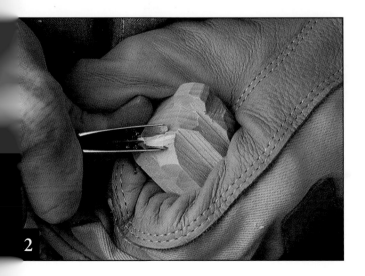

2

Use the 5⁄16" (8mm) V-tool to cut the cheek lines. The mouth and jaw are wide at the bottom and taper in up to the eyebrow. They form a sort of triangle shape, with the point of the triangle coming to a rounded point just below the eye area. Start a shallow cut at the bottom, then apply more pressure to deepen the cut as you make your way to the center of the face. Make several passes, continuing to deepen the cut. Carve both sides of the mouth at the same time to keep the jaw in proportion. Look at the face and make any necessary adjustments to make the jaw or cheek dimensions the same. Remember: Start wide at the bottom and taper in on both sides to form a nice, rounded top on the triangle. The rounded top will form the bridge of the nose under the eyes.

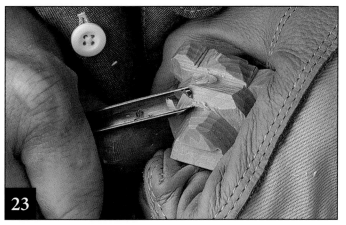

23

Notice the triangle shape of the rounded snout. Clean up the eyebrow just above the snout. Notice my right thumb; I have it planted to control my cuts.

24

Now check the proportions of the face and snout. On the front of the snout, draw the nose. The nose is also a triangle shape, but this time the point of the triangle will point down.

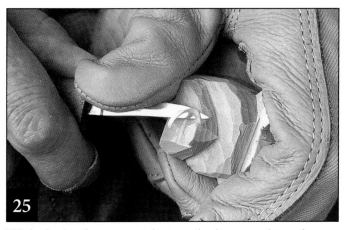

25

With the knife, cut straight into the lines marking the nose. Remove wood on the front of the snout under the nose; then clean up the triangle-shaped nose. Gently round the outside edges of the snout. Don't take off too much wood here.

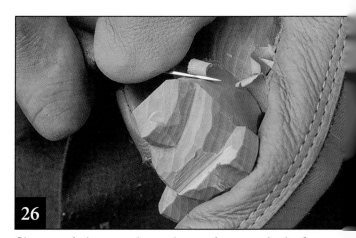

26

Shape and clean up the neck area down to the body. Notice here that I am using my left thumb to pull the blade down the neck. In the next photo, you can see the raised, triangle-shaped nose and the roundness of the snout.

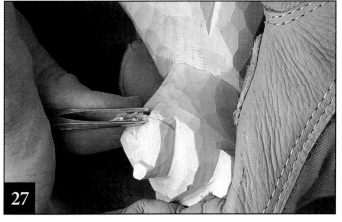

27

Now find the center of the snout. Draw a line to form the droopy jaw. Use a ⅛" (4mm) V-tool to cut the mouth lines. Deepen the cut at the corners of the mouth to tuck in the lower lip.

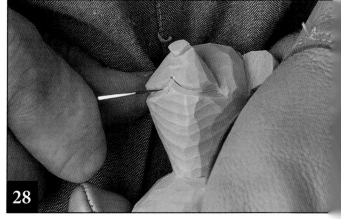

28

With the knife, clean up the corners of the mouth.

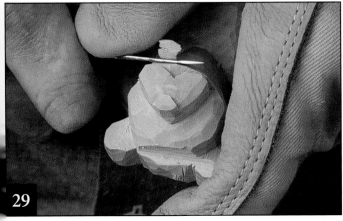

29

Remove the wood on the lower lip to make the jaws jut out over the mouth.

30

Save the ears to last to avoid breaking them. Use the knife to shape the head and the ears. Work on both ears at the same time. Keep checking and comparing the ears. to ensure that both ears are identical.

31

Here I'll pencil some clothes on the bear. We can't have a bare bear!

32

Draw the lines for the overalls on the front, sides, and back of the piece. Use the pattern and the finished photos as guides.

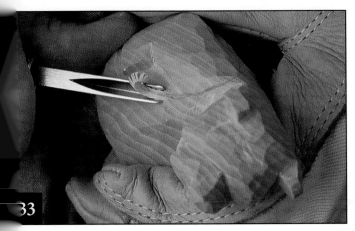

33

Cut the lines defining the overalls with the ⅛" (4mm) V-tool.

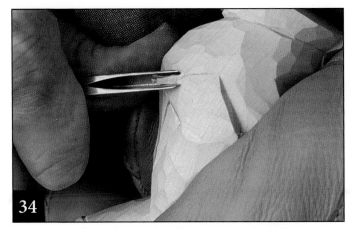

34

Notice the planted thumb. With my thumb in this position, I can start and stop the cut at any point.

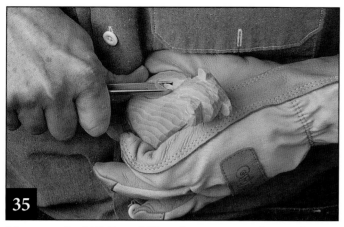

Next use the 5/16" (8mm) V-tool to trim wood away from the overalls. Lay the V-tool flat, away from the overalls, and shave the wood away. These cuts will raise the overalls from the body. Continue cutting around all of the lines for the clothes.

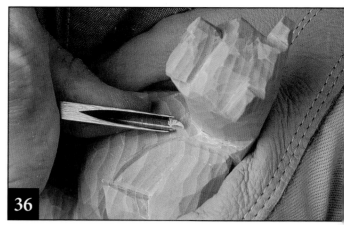

Use the 1/8" (4mm) V-tool to outline the straps. Hold the tool sideways to shave wood away from the straps and raise them up off the overalls.

The 1/8" (4mm) V-tool will be used to complete several steps. First cut the boot soles.

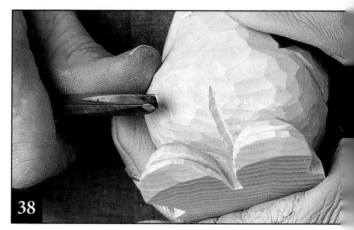

Make the cuts fairly deep so the soles stand out from the shoes.

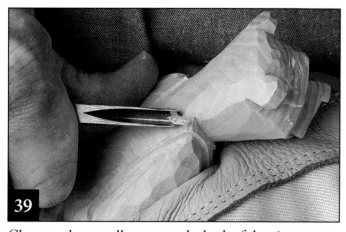

Clean up the overall straps on the back of the piece.

Draw the pockets on the front of the overalls. Cut the lines with the 1/8" (4mm) V-tool.

41

Cut some simple wrinkles around the pant leg cuffs. Wrinkles are made by making simple scoop cuts.

42

Using the same V-tool, make short, random cuts to represent hair lines.

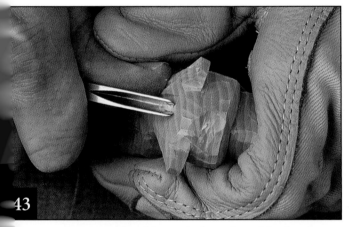

43

These random cuts should vary in length and in depth to give the suggestion of fur.

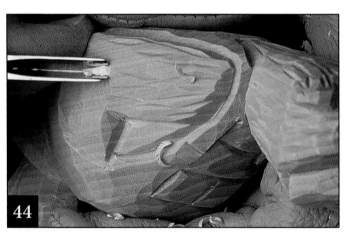

44

Shallow, random cuts are all that is needed to give the appearance of hair or fur. Notice how the carving of the hair is progressing.

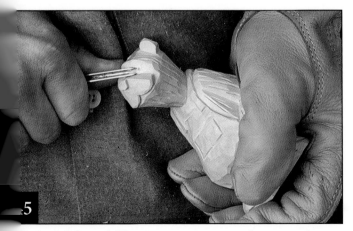

5

Use the ⅛" (3mm) U-gouge to scoop out the eye sockets. Make sure the sockets match before moving on to the next step.

46

Use the same U-gouge to make the eyes. With the open side of the gouge pointed down toward the nose, gently push the gouge straight into the eye socket until you get a distinct U-shaped eye.

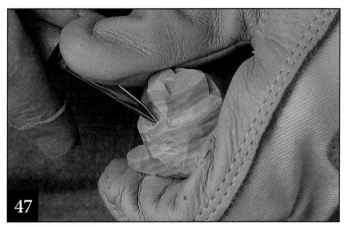

47

Use a detail knife to gently trim the outside edges of the eyeball. All you need to cut is the outside edge of the eyeball. Don't be tempted to carve away any additional wood.

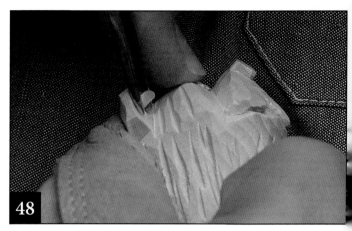

48

Scoop out the insides of the ears with the ⅛" (3mm) U-gouge.

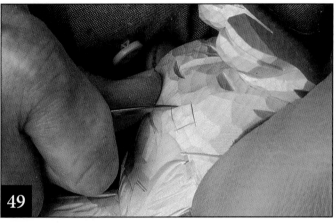

49

With the knife tip, cut some square patches. These patches are simple. Just cut a square and trim away the inside edges of the patch. I usually add three or four patches. You can follow the placement as shown here or place the patches as you desire.

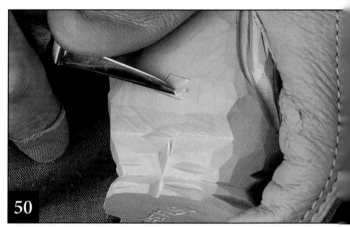

50

The seat of the pants is always a good place for a patch. Notice how the trimmed edges make the patch stand out from the pants.

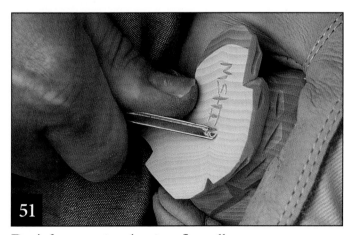

51

Don't forget to sign the piece. I usually carve my signature on the bottom of the carving with a V-tool.

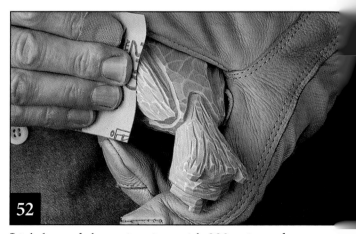

52

Lightly sand the entire piece with 220-grit sandpaper. This will remove any soil from the wood and give the finished piece a worn look. Be careful to sand gently; otherwise, you may find yourself sanding away the tool marks and carved details.

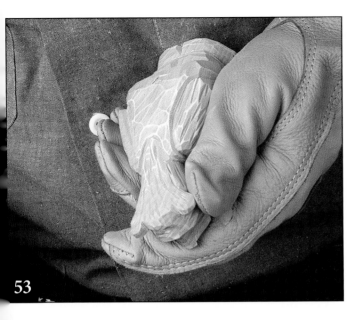

A light sanding will leave the piece looking like this. Notice that you can still see the tool marks and the carved details.

53

54

Make one last check for any last minute adjustments. You'll want to be sure that the finished piece stands properly and that all proportions are correct before you move on to painting.

55

Barry the Bear is finished and ready to paint. It's time to clear away the chips and bring on the paint!

Painting Barry the Bear

As much as I enjoy the actual carving of a piece, I always look forward to painting. Some folks have told me that they like the carving but dread the painting. That feeling is probably the result of their not having enough confidence in their techniques. I think the best way to gain the confidence needed to enjoy painting is to simplify the painting process.

To paint Barry the Bear, I'll show you the technique that I've been using for years. It's the simplest technique I've found.

First, use the common, cheaper acrylic paints that you can buy in any art supply or department store. Acrylics have several advantages: They are inexpensive; they dry quickly; they can be thinned to any shade you want; they can be easily mixed; and they clean up with water. To thin acrylic paints, use approximately 25 percent paint to 75 percent water. This mix will give you a nice wash that allows the grain of the wood to show through. You can increase the strength of the color—for things such as eyes and patches—by adding more paint and less water.

Second, use pure red sable brushes because the bristle tips don't fray. Red sable bristles wear well. They are also flexible enough that they will not flip or spray paint like a stiffer-bristled brush will.

And finally, use circular brush strokes to apply paint to the wood. Never use regular brush strokes to paint a figure because the paint will be darker in one area and lighter in another. I apply the paint to the wood and then blend it over the surface of the wood with circular blending strokes until I have a good, even coat. Of course, in the close areas, I don't load the brush with too much paint. Loading the brush too heavy in a tight spot will cause the colors to bleed into the next area.

Acrylic paints, straight from the tube or thinned with water, are used to paint all the figures in this book.

1

Using a spotter brush, apply thinned white acrylic paint to the eye.

Materials List: Painting Supplies

- #2 shader brush
- #4 shader brush
- #6 shader brush
- Spotter brush
- Paper towels
- Ponce wheel
- Awl
- Toothpicks

Acrylic Paints

- White
- Coffee bean brown
- Tangerine orange
- Charcoal
- Black
- Navy blue
- Burnt umber
- Red
- Yellow
- Orange

2

With a #2 shader, apply thinned tangerine orange to the snout and the insides of the ears.

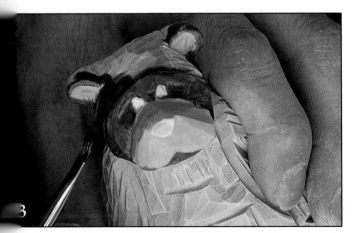

3

Use thinned charcoal black for the fur areas. Even though the paint is thinned, it needs to be black enough to ensure good coverage. Use the #2 shader here around the eyes and ears.

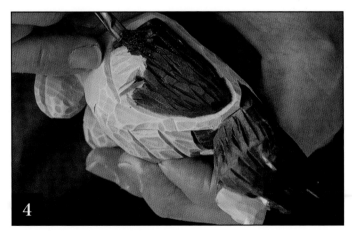

4

On larger areas, like the arms, use a #4 or #6 shader to paint the fur.

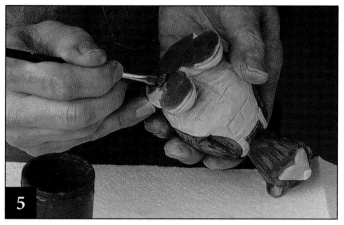

5 Paint the shoes with thinned burnt umber. Use the #6 shader brush.

6 Pause here to allow the colors a few minutes to dry. The progress to this point looks good.

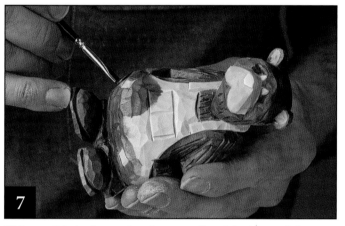

7 Using a #4 shader, paint the overalls with thinned, but strong, navy blue. With any harsh color, like blue or red, you'll need to use circular blending strokes. Keep moving so the painted areas don't have a chance to dry and darken.

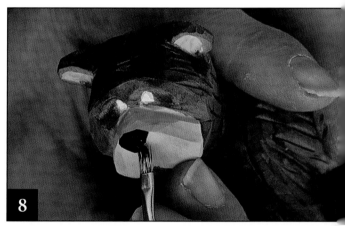

8 Use black straight from the bottle for the nose. A #2 shader works well here.

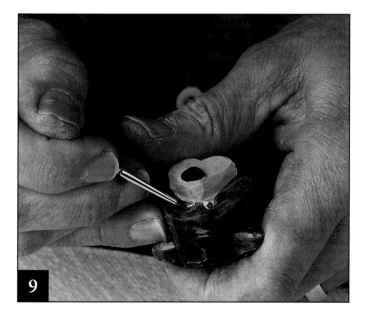

9 Paint the eyes with the spotter brush and coffee bean brown straight from the bottle. Load the tip of the spotter and just touch the eyeball with the paint; then gently expand the eye until it seems to be a realistic size. In a tight spot like this it is easy to slip. The little finger on my right hand is firmly planted for stability.

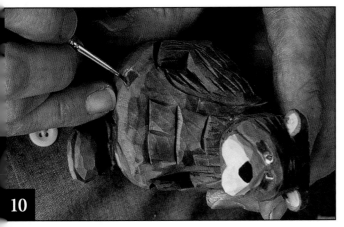

10

Use the spotter to paint the patches. I used thinned red, yellow, and orange, but you can choose any combination of colors for your bear.

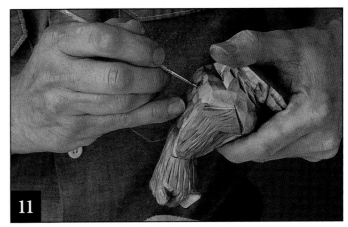

11

Here is an example of a finished patch. This orange patch appears on the seat of the bear's overalls.

12

After the paint dries on the patches, use a pounce wheel to cut the stitches around the edges of the patches. Rolling the wheel and applying slight pressure makes nice-looking stitch holes.

13

Dip a toothpick in white paint straight from the bottle and dot the upper highlight on the brown eye. Notice how this makes the eye more lifelike. Repeat this process on the opposite eye.

4

Cut the tip off a toothpick and load it with white paint. Lightly touch the overall straps with the toothpick to make white buttons.

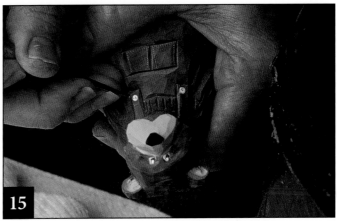

15

Allow the white buttons to dry for a minute; then punch buttonholes with the awl. The painted piece will need to dry for approximately one hour before staining.

Antiquing Barry the Bear

As we all know, there are many finishes that can be used on a carved and painted piece. My favorite finish is boiled linseed oil with a small amount of raw umber oil paint. To make a small amount of this stain, use a large peanut butter jar filled with boiled linseed oil and add a 1" (2.5cm) long ribbon of raw umber oil paint straight from the tube. Shake the mixture well before each use.

Before applying this finish, notice how the acrylic colors have a dry, harsh look. This linseed oil mix will soften the colors and give the piece an instant antique appearance. This finish will also make the piece practically water resistant. My wife actually washed some of my old, dusty pieces under the kitchen faucet with no sign of danger to the wood.

This finish can be brushed on. However, I prefer dipping the piece directly in the mix because it's much faster. As you can see in the following photos, I have a bucket full of this mixture. I mix large batches with an old kitchen blender. Be sure to work in a well-ventilated area.

Materials List: Staining Supplies
- Boiled linseed oil
- Raw umber oil paint
- Paper towels

1

Mix the stain well; then, holding the piece between the thumb and forefinger of one hand, dip half of the carved and painted piece into the stain.

2

Now quickly dip the other half of the piece and allow the excess to drip off. Towel the piece dry with paper towels. Dispose of the stain-soaked towels (they are combustible!) according to your local ordinances to avoid a fire hazard. The piece may feel a little greasy or tacky after towel drying, but that will disappear in a few hours. The smell will disappear in about 24 hours.

Whittling the Country Bear & His Friends

Part Three

Projects

Now that you've carved, painted, and stained Barry, it's time to make some friends for him. I have designed a forest full of animals to keep him company. On the following pages you'll find photos and patterns for 11 additional projects. Each project includes ready-to-use patterns and photographs of the finished pieces. The patterns are scaled to match Barry's proportions but can be enlarged or reduced to any size. Carving tips and

photos of the unfinished pieces are included to keep you from getting stumped along the way.

All of Barry's friends can be completed with the tools listed in the Getting Started section of this book. A list of recommended colors and painting materials accompanies each project. The finishing technique for each of these pieces is the same. Simply use the staining method described in the Step-by-Step Instructions section.

Christmas Bear

The Christmas Bear keeps the Christmas spirit alive in the forest all year long. Based on the same pattern as Barry the Bear, this carving makes a good second project for a beginning carver. Simply follow the step-by-step instructions for Barry and allow extra wood for the Christmas Bear's hat.

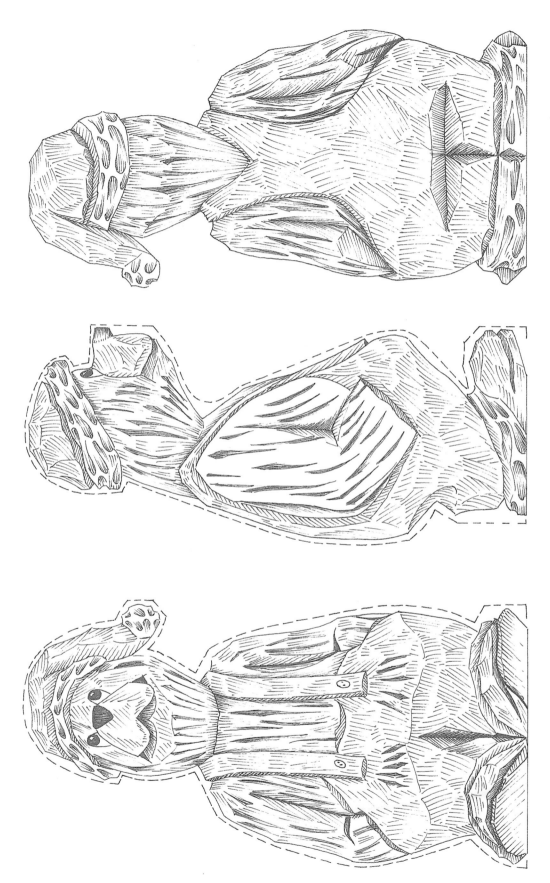

Materials List:

- Spotter brush
- #2 shader brush
- #4 shader brush
- #6 shader brush
- Toothpicks

Acrylic Paints

- White
- Coffee bean brown
- Tangerine orange
- Black
- Charcoal black
- Burnt umber
- Opaque red

The Christmas Bear is a modified version of the step-by-step bear. Use the same carving and painting techniques as explained in the step-by-step instructions section of this book. The only exception is his red and white Santa hat.

The overalls are penciled on with the straps going over the shoulders.

Take note of the depth of the arm and the side profile of the head.

Here the tassel is roughed in. The tassel is rounded to the right size.

Patriotic Bear

As you can see, even the forest has its own Uncle Sam. Again, this bear is simply another version of the step-by-step bear. This time, I've added a top hat and changed his clothing to a jacket and pants. You can continue to add other bears to the forest by making similar changes of your own.

Patriotic Bear

Whittling the Country Bear & His Friends

Materials List:

- Spotter brush
- #2 shader brush
- #4 shader brush
- #6 shader brush
- Toothpicks

Acrylic Paints

- Coffee bean brown
- White
- Tangerine orange
- Black
- Charcoal black
- Burnt umber
- Opaque red
- Navy blue
- Bright yellow

The stars and the stripes on this bear will need a little extra care. To make the stars, use white acrylic straight from the bottle. Load the tip of the toothpick and dot the wood; then drag paint out from the center of the dot to make a five-pointed star. You can practice making stars on a scrap piece of wood, but keep in mind that the stars don't have to be perfect. To make the stripes, use a spotter brush. Remember to plant your fingers to steady your hand.

Compare this bear with the Christmas Bear and Barry the Bear. You'll notice that he is carved from basically the same pattern. Only the clothes and the hat are different.

Everything is roughed in except the hat. Notice the penciled line on the hat brim. Cut this line with a 5/16" (8mm) V-tool. Deepen the cut as you follow it around until you have a good brim width. Take care with the brim; as you deepen the cut, the brim will become more and more fragile.

Cut the penciled lines on the back of the coat to make the belt and the coat tails. Use a 1/8" (4mm) V-tool to cut the coat sleeve cuffs and the pant leg cuffs.

Pa Bear

Old Pa Bear probably spends most of his time looking for those cubs hidden in the hollow tree. This is another variation on the step-by-step bear. The pattern for this fellow was simply stretched out to make him taller than his oldest son, Barry. Notice that I didn't just enlarge the pattern. Pa Bear's face and body are actually much thinner than Barry's, a result of the "stretching."

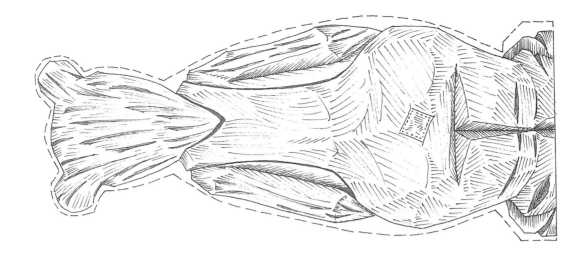

Pa Bear

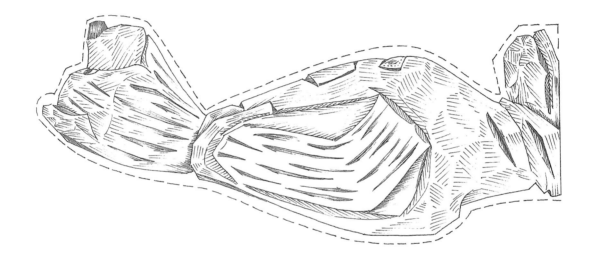

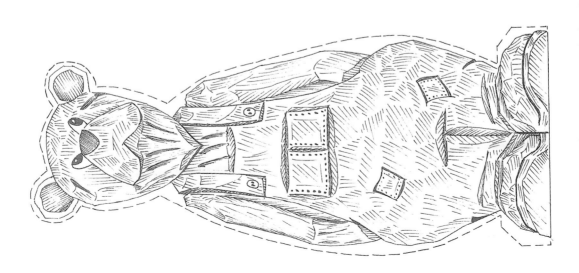

Materials List:

- Spotter brush
- #2 shader brush
- #4 shader brush
- #6 shader brush
- Toothpicks

Acrylic Paints

- White
- Coffee bean brown
- Tangerine orange
- Black
- Charcoal black
- Navy blue
- Burnt umber
- Yellow
- Red
- Green

The same painting steps shown in the step-by-step project apply here; this bear is just a little slimmer and taller.

You can reduce or enlarge this pattern to make a bear of any size.

At this point everything is roughed in and ready for some details. Here's a good side view of the head and the arm depth.

The back of the piece is finished, except fo cutting the overalls lines and separating the legs.

Ma Bear

Ma Bear probably spends most of her time looking for Pa Bear. Again, you can see the similarities between this carving and the step-by-step carving. Ma's dress covers her back paws, which makes her a little easier to carve than the other bears. She is also wearing a hat that covers her ears as well.

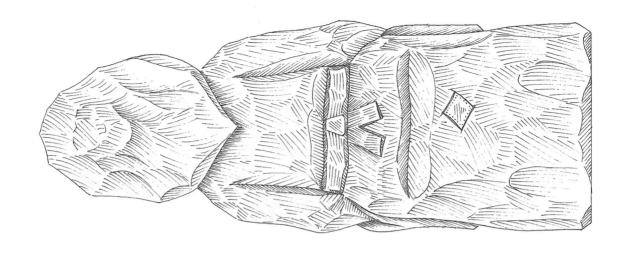

Ma Bear

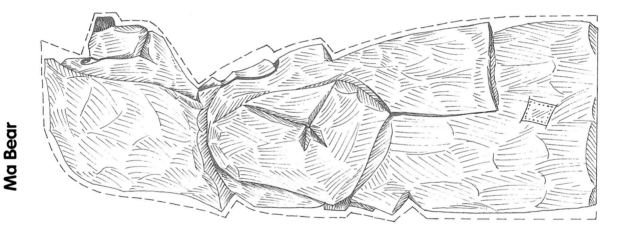

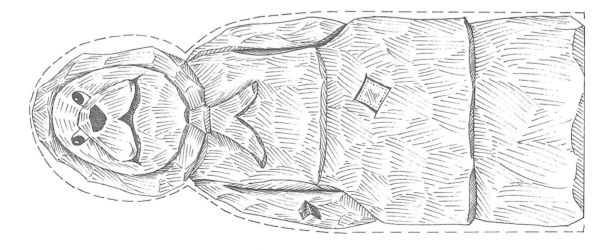

Materials List:

- Spotter brush
- #2 shader brush
- #4 shader brush
- #6 shader brush
- Toothpicks

Acrylic Paints

- White
- Coffee bean brown
- Tangerine orange
- Black
- Charcoal black
- Navy blue
- Yellow
- Red
- Hunter green

I've listed the colors that I used to paint Ma Bear, but you can mix and match just about any color on this piece. The apron strings on the back of the piece and the patches add a bit of character and interest to Ma Bear's outfit. Take note that the apron strings come together in a simple knot with the two ends flowing down from the knot.

re's a change of pace—for this bear, don't need to carve the ears. But a's hat is a little bit of a challenge. e details are penciled in.

The hat is just a bonnet-style scarf that flows to the shoulders. The side view shows the arm shape and depth. The arm just disappears under the apron.

Clean up the rear of the dress before carving the apron strings.

Cub in a Stump

This guy has that look of mischief about him. There's no telling what he's been up to, but it looks like he's found a good hiding place. Poor Pa Bear may never find him in there.

Cub in a Stump

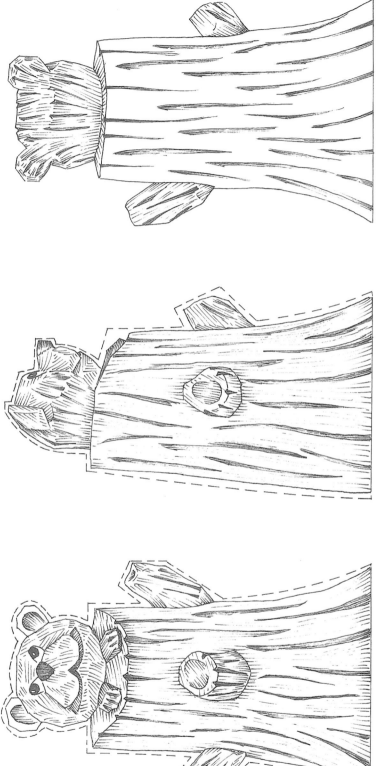

© 2003 Mike Shipley. **Shown Actual Size.** Dashed line indicates saw cutout.

Materials List:

- Spotter brush
- #2 shader brush
- #4 shader brush
- #6 shader brush
- Toothpicks

Acrylic Paints

- White
- Coffee bean brown
- Black
- Charcoal black
- Tangerine orange
- Burnt umber

The colors on the head need to be nice and bright to offset the burnt umber used on the stump. Notice how the limb stumps give the carving a little character. You can change the look of the project by making the stump taller.

As you can see from this photo, everything is carved down and ready for detail. I penciled in the facial features and the front paws resting on the stump.

Notice the thickness of the ears. That's about the right thickness in relation to the head. The ears point forward slightly.

Use the ⅛" (4mm) V-tool to carve the bark lines on the stump. These are short, random cuts that will give the appearance of tree bark.

Double Trouble

I wonder if these two realize that they have company in this old hollow tree. I'll let you decide who the mystery guest is.

Double Trouble

Whittling the Country Bear & His Friends

Materials List:

- Spotter brush
- #2 shader brush
- #4 shader brush
- #6 shader brush
- Toothpicks

Acrylic Paints

- White
- Coffee bean brown
- Black
- Charcoal black
- Burnt umber

The dark hole in the tree can be placed anywhere you like. Drill the hole with a ½" (13mm) drill bit, ⅜" to ½" (1 to 1.3cm) deep. Paint the hole with straight black. Use a blunt toothpick to dot the white eyes; then make a smaller dot with coffee bean brown. Use a sharp toothpick to place a tiny white dot on the brown eyes. Another hole can be carved on the backside of the tree.

e fork in the tree makes this piece a little ficult to carve, but the effect is worth it.

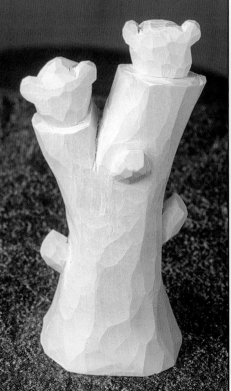

Don't try to match the size or the appearance of the cubs. It is perfectly all right if they're not the same size and don't look identical.

The cub on the right side is harder to carve because he is lower and because you can't give him any band sawed detail when you saw the blank. I find it best to carve the bear cub on the higher branch first.

Well-Dressed Moose

What we have here is your typical, everyday, well-dressed moose. Just because you live out in the forest is no excuse not to look your best.

Well-Dressed Moose

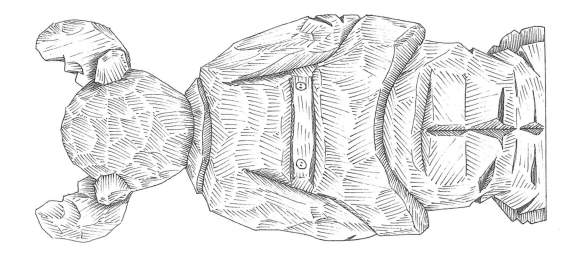

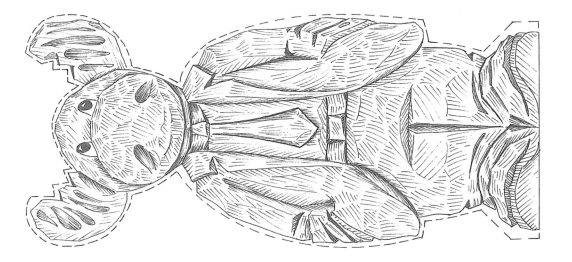

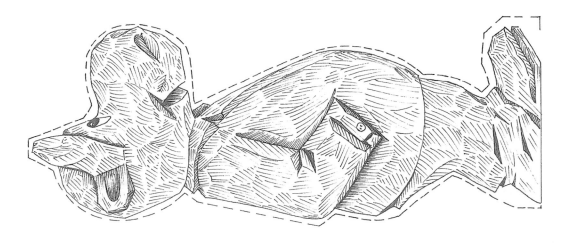

Materials List:

- Spotter brush
- #2 shader brush
- #4 shader brush
- #6 shader brush
- Toothpicks

Acrylic Paints

- White
- Coffee bean brown
- Charcoal black
- Navy Blue
- Burnt umber

On this piece, the antlers are the most difficult area to carve. Take it slow and easy, leaving the antlers thick until all of the other carving work is completed. You'll have less chance of breaking an antler if you wait to thin them down when the rest of the piece is done. If you do break an antler, don't despair. A little wood glue will take care of the problem.

At this point all of the main features are established. Finish everything else before you carve the antlers. As you work the antlers down to their finished size, they will become more delicate and will break easily.

Notice the antlers' thickness as compared to the head. Thin them down with a detail knife after all of the other carving is done. Don't worry about getting all of the antler points to match; they can have a random look.

Take note of the short ears behind the antlers. The ears are just short and simpl with a scoop to indicate the insides. Agai be careful of the antlers as you carve the ears.

Do-Nothin' Rabbit

This bunny just kind of blends in around the forest and does whatever it is that rabbits do. Because there are no predators in this forest, he pretty much has it made. This is a good thing, considering the fact that he doesn't look too alert standing there with his hands in his pockets.

Do-Nothin' Rabbit

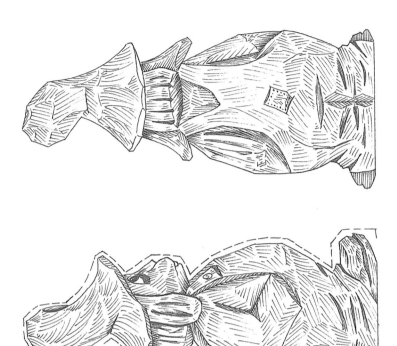

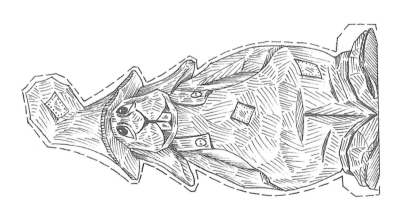

Materials List:

- Spotter brush
- #2 shader brush
- #4 shader brush
- Toothpicks

Acrylic Paints

- White
- Coffee bean brown
- Charcoal black
- Navy Blue
- Red
- Yellow
- Orange
- Green

The same process used to cut the fur, or hair lines, on the bear projects can be used here. Simply make short, varied cuts with a ⅛" (4mm) V-tool. The same tool can be used to cut wrinkles in the pant legs. Wrinkles in the clothing add character and interest to the piece.

...his photo shows the halfway point. The ...t needs some work and the other shoe ...eds to be finished. The face and teeth are ...nciled in.

Notice how the ears are roughed in. On this side the arm still needs to be finished.

Finish the backside by cutting the arm lines with the V-tool. Clean up the area with a knife.

Busy Beaver

Meet the construction foreman of the forest. This is one progressive beaver. He has found out that the ax is mightier than the teeth. Apparently he hasn't yet heard of that invention called the chainsaw.

Busy Beaver

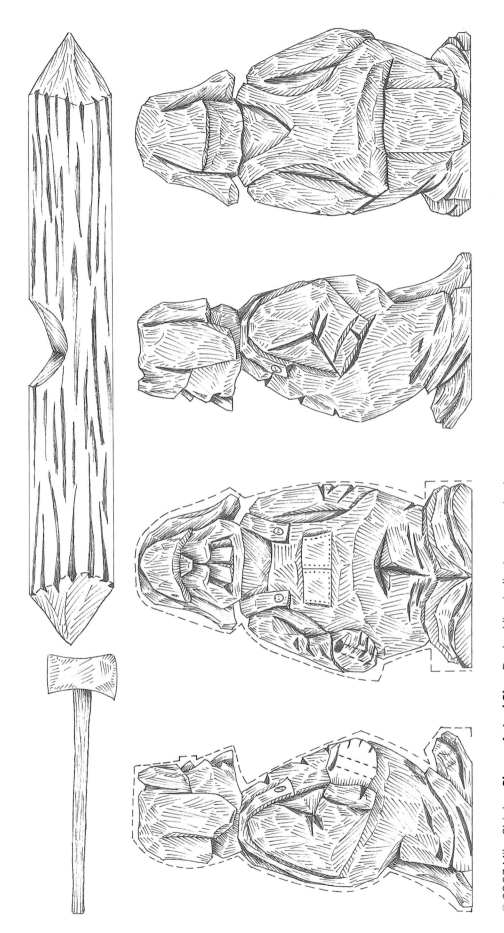

Materials List:

- Spotter brush
- #2 shader brush
- #4 shader brush
- Toothpicks

Acrylic Paints

- White
- Burnt umber
- Coffee bean brown
- Navy blue
- Thicket green
- Red
- Silver

The log that the beaver has been working on is just a ¾" x ¾" (2 x 2cm) piece of wood carved into a cylindrical shape and detailed with a V-tool. Paint the log burnt umber and leave the chopped areas natural. The fur is painted coffee bean brown; the shoes and tail are burnt umber. A few patches might add some character to this piece. To finish the ax, leave the handle unpainted and paint the ax head silver.

In this photo, we're ready to finish the shoes and work on the face and those big teeth. Notice how the hat rests on the nose and covers the eyes.

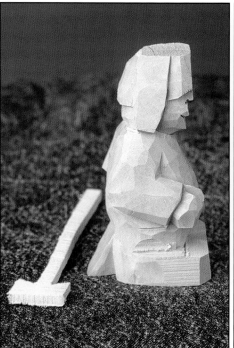

Drill a ⅛" (0.3cm) hole through the hand; then carve the ax handle to fit the hole.

The flat tail will just appear to come out of the seat of his pants.

Forest Trees

We've got a forest theme going here, so we've got to have some trees. These trees are really fun and easy to carve, and they add a great effect if you want to do a grouping with the animals. The large photo on this page shows the beaver grouped with two trees and his hewn log. You can also reduce or enlarge the trees to any size.

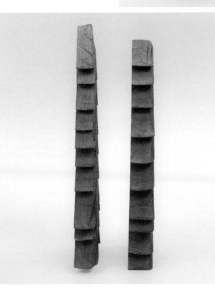

Forest Trees

© 2003 Mike Shipley. **Shown Actual Size**.

Whittling the Country Bear & His Friends

© 2003 Mike Shipley. **Shown Actual Size**.

Materials List:

- #6 shader brush
- #8 shader brush

Acrylic Paints

- Thicket Green
- Burnt Umber

Mix the thicket green very strong to get a good, deep green. Paint the base of the tree with burnt umber. Notice I've added some random cuts on the branches. These were made with the ⅛" (4mm) V-tool at my discretion. You can carve as much or as little detail into the front of these trees as you like. The backside remains uncarved.

Notice the deep undercuts under each branch. Make these cuts with the ⁵⁄₁₆" (8mm) V-tool. Cleanup under the branches is done with a knife.

The backside of the tree does not have the undercuts. It is left plain. Sand both sides with a belt sander.

To create those deep undercuts, lay the V-tool on its side away from the branch that you are undercutting. You can cut in a downward stroke like this, or you can cut up into the tree. Here I am cutting downward. Deepen each cut as you cut from the interior of the tree to the end of the limbs. Clean up the area with the kn

More Great Books from Fox Chapel Publishing

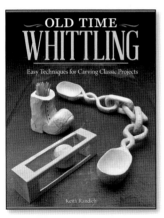

Old Time Whittling
ISBN 978-1-56523-774-2 **$9.99**

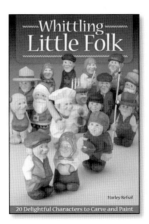

Whittling Little Folk
ISBN 978-1-56523-518-2 **$16.95**

Lurecraft
ISBN 978-1-56523-780-3 **$19.99**

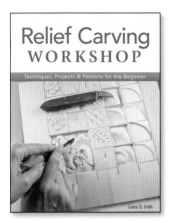

Relief Carving Workshop
ISBN 978-1-56523-736-0 **$19.99**

Chip Carving Workshop
ISBN 978-1-56523-776-6 **$16.99**

Learn to Burn
ISBN 978-1-56523-728-5 **$16.99**

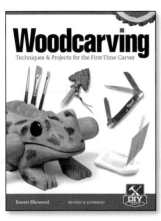

**Woodcarving,
Revised and Expanded**
ISBN 978-1-56523-800-8 **$14.99**

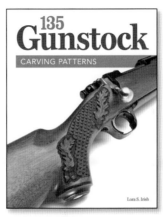

135 Gunstock Carving Patterns
ISBN 978-1-56523-795-7 **$16.99**

**Relief Carving Wood Spirits,
Revised Edition**
ISBN 978-1-56523-802-2 **$19.99**

More Great Books from Fox Chapel Publishing

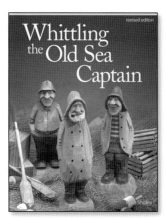

Whittling the Old Sea Captain, Revised Edition
ISBN 978-1-56523-815-2 **$12.99**

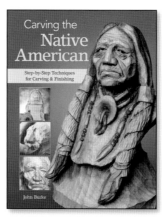

Carving the Native American
ISBN 978-1-56523-787-2 **$19.99**

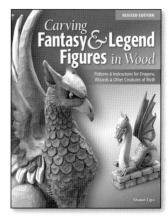

Carving Fantasy & Legend Figures in Wood, Revised Edition
ISBN 978-1-56523-807-7 **$19.99**

Big Book of Whittle Fun
ISBN 978-1-56523-520-5 **$12.95**

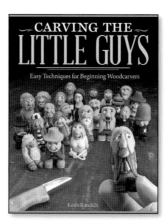

Carving the Little Guys
ISBN 978-1-56523-775-9 **$9.99**

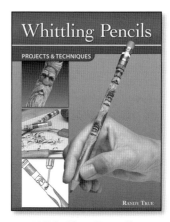

Whittling Pencils
ISBN 978-1-56523-751-3 **$12.99**

WOODCARVING
ILLUSTRATED

In addition to being a leading source of woodworking books and DVDs, Fox Chapel also publishes *Woodcarving Illustrated*. Released quarterly, it delivers premium projects, expert tips and techniques from today's finest carvers, and in-depth information about the latest tools, equipment, and materials.

Subscribe Today!
Woodcarving Illustrated: **888-506-6630**
www.FoxChapelPublishing.com